W9-BBZ-475

WITHDRAWN

WALLINGFORD PUBLIC LIBRARY
200 North Main St.
Wallingford, CT 06492

SCIENCE EXPLORER

CHILDREN'S LIBRARY

UNDERSTANDING
INSECTS

Follow the Clues

by Tamra B. Orr

WALLINGFORD PUBLIC LIBRARY
200 North Main St.
Wallingford, CT 06492

CHERRY LAKE PUBLISHING · ANN ARBOR, MICHIGAN

This book is intended to introduce readers to the Next Generation Science Standards (NGSS). These standards emphasize a general set of eight practices for scientific investigation, rather than a rigid set of steps. Keywords taken from the NGSS are highlighted in the text. The eight science practices are:

1. Asking questions
2. Developing and using models
3. Planning and carrying out investigations
4. Analyzing and interpreting data
5. Using mathematics and computational thinking
6. Constructing explanations
7. Engaging in argument from evidence
8. Obtaining, evaluating, and communicating information

Published in the United States of America by Cherry Lake Publishing
Ann Arbor, Michigan
www.cherrylakepublishing.com

CONTENT EDITOR: Melissa Miller, Next Generation Science Standards Writer, Science Teacher, Farmington, Arkansas
BOOK DESIGN AND ILLUSTRATION: The Design Lab
READING ADVISER: Marla Conn, Readability, Inc.

PHOTO CREDITS: Cover and page 1, ©Amir Ridhwan/Shutterstock, Inc.; page 4, ©ZanozaRu/Shutterstock, Inc.; page 5, ©Bork/Shutterstock, Inc.; page 6, ©Bork/Shutterstock, Inc.; page 7, ©bierchen/Shutterstock, Inc.; page 8, ©skynetphoto/Shutterstock, Inc.; page 9, ©Juniors Bildarchiv GmbH/Alamy; page 10, ©jack thomas/Alamy; page 11, ©jack thomas/Alamy; page 12, ©Alexey Stiop/Shutterstock, Inc.; page 13, ©James Allen/Alamy; page 14, ©Tyler Olson/Shutterstock, Inc.; page 15, ©Tyler Olson/Shutterstock, Inc.; page 16, ©Jsimsphoto/Dreamstime.com; page 17, ©ARENA Creative/Shutterstock, Inc.; page 18, ©Zhiltsov Alexandr/Shutterstock, Inc.; page 19, ©_David Gee/Alamy; page 20, ©romakoma/Shutterstock, Inc.; page 21, ©Simon Krzic/Dreamstime.com; page 22, ©sakhorn/Shutterstock, Inc.; page 23, ©National Geographic Image Collection/Alamy; page 24, © Kypros/Alamy; page 25, ©Gladskikh Tatiana/Shutterstock, Inc.; page 26, ©Joerg Boethling/Alamy; page 27, ©RGB Ventures LLC dba SuperStock/Alamy; page 28, ©MShieldsPhotos/Alamy; page 29, ©Staphy/Dreamstime.com.

Copyright ©2014 by Cherry Lake Publishing
All rights reserved. No part of this book may be reproduced or utilized in any form or by any means without written permission from the publisher.

LIBRARY OF CONGRESS CATALOGING-IN-PUBLICATION DATA
Orr, Tamra, author.
Understanding insects / by Tamra B. Orr.
pages cm. — (Science explorer. Follow the clues)
Audience: Grades 4 to 6.
Summary: "Use the next generation science standards to learn how insects can transmit diseases."—Provided by publisher.
Includes bibliographical references and index.
ISBN 978-1-62431-783-5 (lib. bdg.) — ISBN 978-1-62431-793-4 (pbk.) — ISBN 978-1-62431-813-9 (ebook) — ISBN 978-1-62431-803-0 (pdf)
1. Mosquitoes as carriers of disease—Juvenile literature. 2. Insects as carriers of disease—Juvenile literature. 3. Mosquitoes—Control—Juvenile literature. I. Title.

RA640.O77 2014
614.4'32—dc23   2013042108

Cherry Lake Publishing would like to acknowledge the work of The Partnership for 21st Century Skills. Please visit www.p21.org for more information.

Printed in the United States of America, Corporate Graphics Inc.
January 2014

TABLE OF CONTENTS

CHAPTER 1

STANDING WATER, BE GONE!

Mosquitoes thrive in hot, moist conditions.

Tomás slapped his arm for what felt like the one-hundredth time in the last 10 minutes. Darn mosquitoes! They sure knew how to ruin a backyard picnic. As he scratched at the red bump forming on his arm, Tomás saw his neighbor Mr. Woodson scratching his own arm.

"There are a lot of those biters out tonight," said Mr. Woodson.

Mrs. Woodson studied the bites on her husband's arm. "We're not bit nearly as much when we visit the Littletons," she said, nodding toward

Tomás and his mother, Lily. "There just seem to be more mosquitoes around our house."

"Why do we have more mosquitoes than Tomás and Lily?" her husband asked.

"It's a great question," said Mrs. Littleton. "There could be a few different reasons. The first way to deal with those pesky insects is to make sure there is no standing water around."

Tomás, Mrs. Littleton, and the Woodsons looked around. After last night's heavy rainfall, there was plenty of water around the Woodsons' house. Tomás noticed three clay flowerpots filled with water. There was

A scientist inspects a tick inside a glass vial.

also a puddle inside the garden's wheelbarrow and several inches of water in a plastic bucket. Mr. Woodson pointed out a couple of pet dishes full of water, too.

"Is standing water the only thing we need to worry about?" Mrs. Woodson asked.

Tomás thought about the class his mom taught at the community college. As an **entomologist**, she never ran away from bugs. Instead, she caught them and studied them! She probably knew a bunch of ways to keep mosquitoes away.

"Why don't we do an experiment?" asked Tomás. "We can use science to figure out why mosquitoes like the Woodsons' yard so much. Mom, I'm sure you have some ideas we can try."

Mosquitoes often gather in places where there is standing water.

Many insects are attracted to bright lights at night.

"As a matter of fact, I do!" Mrs. Littleton answered with a smile.

Mr. Woodson clapped his hands together happily. "Let's come up with a plan," he said. "We should start with a **baseline** study. We'll collect information on how many mosquitoes visit each of our yards in 24 hours. Then we can try some of Lily's other ideas for keeping out those pesky bugs. We'll do another study afterward to see how well those ideas worked."

"I have light traps we can use to catch the mosquitoes over the next 24 hours," said Mrs. Littleton. "We can set one in each of our yards. Tomorrow night, we can check how many mosquitoes each trap caught."

"I'll run and get them now!" said Tomás.

"Hold on, Tomás," said Mrs. Woodson, putting a hand on Tomás's arm. "Let's move this picnic inside, away from the mosquitoes, and enjoy our meal first!"

CHASING AFTER BUGS

Jewel bug

What is the largest group of animals in the world? If you said insects, you're right! In fact, 80 percent of all known animals on Earth are insects! Experts have identified about one million species, but there may be as many as 30 million more waiting to be discovered.

Entomologists collect specimens, or samples, in the field to study. Often, this involves using light. Many insects are attracted to light and naturally fly toward it. Insects may then be collected with a sheet or a bucket, net, or other container.

Scientists study each individual insect. They record what type of insect it is, where it was collected, and when it was collected. Entomologists often share this information with other experts and anyone else who is interested. These people can use the information as background research or as evidence in their own studies.

CHAPTER 2

INFORMED INVESTIGATORS

Huge numbers of mosquitoes can thrive in a small area if the conditions are just right.

The next evening, Tomás and his mother returned to help the Woodsons count how many mosquitoes had been caught.

Mrs. Woodson wrinkled her nose. "I had no idea we had so many mosquitoes." She recorded the number on a notepad.

"Keep in mind that the trap didn't catch all of the mosquitoes in your yard," Mrs. Littleton pointed out. "May I borrow your notepad, Ella?" Mrs. Woodson handed over the notepad and pencil. Mrs. Littleton

Mosquito larvae hang just below the surface of standing water.

scribbled some numbers on the paper, doing a few calculations. "We had about one-third the number of mosquitoes in our yard."

"Then you must be doing something correctly," said Mr. Woodson. "We need to learn more information about mosquitoes so we can figure out how to stop them."

"What do mosquitoes need to survive?" Mrs. Woodson asked. "I think if we take those things away, the insects will be less likely to visit our yard."

"You're exactly right," said Mrs. Littleton. "First of all, mosquito **larvae** hatch and grow in standing water. Rid your yard of that, and mosquitoes won't be able to breed here.

"Also, female mosquitoes feed on the blood of people and animals," Mrs. Littleton continued. "A female uses the blood to feed the eggs that are inside her body. It is the only way she can make babies. You can keep her from biting you by covering your body with long sleeves and pants. Put mosquito **repellent** on your skin, and also spray it on your clothing. Read the directions on the repellent so you know how often to reapply it."

"Insects hate the smell of citronella, too," said Tomás. "You can buy citronella candles and light them when you're going to be outside. You can make your own candles, too. That's what Mom and I did, and it was fun."

Mrs. Woodson wrote down all of these tips on her notepad. "Anything else?" she asked.

Bug spray is a great way to keep insects away from your body.

Mrs. Littleton thought for a moment. "Insects like to hide in long grass. You can mow your lawn regularly to cut down on that." Mrs. Woodson wrote this down, too.

Mr. Woodson looked over his wife's shoulder. "Quite the list," he said. "Now what?"

"Let's find all the standing water in our yards and measure how tall the grass is," Tomás responded. "We can also count our citronella candles. I know Mom and I have two."

Mrs. Woodson smiled. "This sounds like a scavenger hunt!"

Mowing tall grass is one way to keep mosquitoes away from your yard.

"Mom, where is Skeeter?" Tomás asked.

"On a shelf in the upstairs closet," replied Mrs. Littleton. "Why?"

"I think we might need to explain mosquitoes a little more in general to the Woodsons. Skeeter might help," Tomás said.

Tomás went to get Skeeter, a large plastic model of a mosquito. Mrs. Littleton had many specimens, as well as big models like Skeeter. She used them to teach Tomás and her students about insects' bodies and how insects grow and reproduce.

When they went to the Woodsons', Tomás placed Skeeter on the table.

"Mosquitoes have three main body parts. The first part is the head," he said, holding up the piece. "It has two large eyes. It also has two **antennae**, which are used to hear and smell." Pointing to a long, needlelike tube on the front of the head, he added, "This is the mosquito's mouth, which makes the bite. It is called a **proboscis**."

Mrs. Littleton picked up the next large piece. "This is the **thorax**," she said. "Six of the insect's legs and its wings are attached to it." She picked up the last piece. "The final body part of the mosquito is called the **abdomen**. This is where the stomach is. The holes on the side are used for breathing."

CHAPTER 3

MAPPING OUT, CLEANING UP

↖ Tomás drew a map of his family's yard.

"Hi, Lily and Tomás," said Mr. Woodson as he opened his front door for them the next day.

Mrs. Woodson welcomed the Littletons as they came inside. "What's in the bag, Tomás?" she asked.

They all went into the Woodsons' kitchen, and Tomás emptied the contents of the bag he was carrying. "I have two sketch pads, pencils, and two rulers. We'll use the paper and pencils to draw maps of our yards. The rulers are so we can measure the grass in different places around the yards."

The two families mapped out their yards on separate pieces of paper. On each map, they marked the locations of the house and driveway. Mrs. Littleton kept a garden, so she added that to her map. Mr. Woodson had a small shed in the yard, so that was added to his map.

Next, everyone went outside. "There are many places to find standing water on a property," Mrs. Littleton explained. She pulled a list out of her pocket and showed it to the others.

Birdbaths
Boats
Buckets
Drainage ditches
Lawn furniture
Old tires
Pet dishes
Plastic sheeting
Plugged roof gutters

Ponds
Potted plants with pans
Puddles in low areas
Trash cans
Wading pools
Watering cans
Wheelbarrows

For the next 45 minutes, they searched for standing water in the Woodsons' yard. When they found some, they marked it on the map. Tomás and Mrs. Woodson measured the grass in a few places near the house, in the middle of the yard, and at the yard's edge. They added these figures to the map, marking where they had taken each measurement. When they were done, everyone went to the Littletons' yard and did the same thing. Mrs. Littleton marked the location of a puddle she had found.

"Don't forget to add our two citronella candles on the map," Tomás told his mom.

Many people use citronella torches to help keep insects away from their yards.

Citronella candles often come in large buckets so they can burn for a long time.

"Actually, there are three," said Mr. Woodson, pointing toward the Littletons' porch. "One at each end of your porch and one more in the center." Mrs. Littleton drew little circles on the map to show where the citronella candles were.

When both maps were finished, Tomás, his mother, and the Woodsons went inside to the Littletons' kitchen. Mrs. Woodson studied the maps, analyzing their differences. "The grass is at about the same height in both of our yards. We have a lot more standing water in our yard, though. Plus, you have those candles on your porch. We don't have any citronella."

Long-sleeved shirts can help prevent mosquito bites by keeping the insects away from your skin.

"It seems to me," said Mr. Woodson, "that it's time we made some changes, Ella."

"Excellent point," Mrs. Woodson responded. "Let's get rid of all of that standing water and find some citronella candles."

"We can pick up some mosquito repellent, too, and some long-sleeved shirts. I want as few mosquitoes to bite me as possible," Mr. Woodson added. "We can all check back in a week and see how our mosquito population has changed."

A nurse checks on a dengue fever patient in India.

Mosquitoes and other insects can spread diseases. Scientists can learn a lot about a disease by comparing data. They can figure out why the disease might flourish in one place but not another, or why it infects one group of people more often than others. Some diseases are common only at certain times of year. Looking at what makes that season different from other seasons can also provide information about a disease.

For instance, certain mosquitoes can spread dengue fever. This disease causes pain in the muscles and joints, a skin rash, and sometimes death. While dengue fever has become a leading cause of death in areas of Latin America and South Asia, it is extremely rare in North America. Why? Scientists found a key reason: climate. Dengue fever occurs in the tropics and subtropics, where the climate is warm and wet. Certain species of mosquitoes thrive in these areas. Through further study, scientists were able to determine exactly what species of mosquitoes spreads dengue fever.

CHAPTER 4

SEEING RESULTS

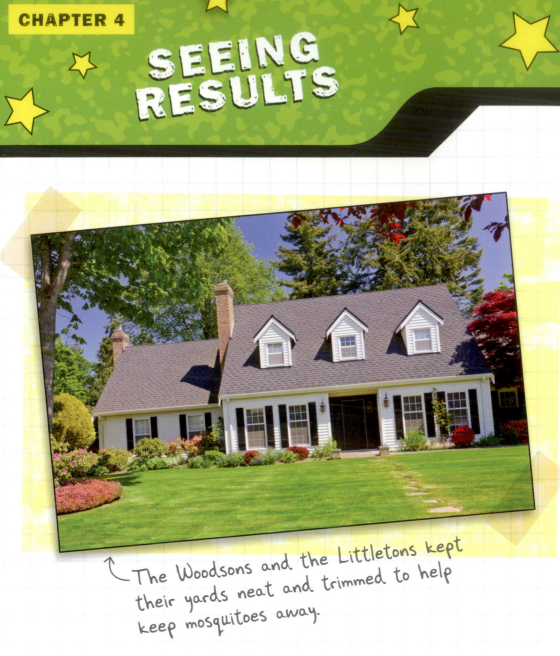

The Woodsons and the Littletons kept their yards neat and trimmed to help keep mosquitoes away.

Over the next week, the Woodsons and the Littletons mowed their lawns regularly. They kept their yards clear of standing water as much as possible. The Woodsons also bought citronella candles and placed them around their porch. If Mr. Woodson went to his shed in the evening, he made sure to wear long sleeves and some mosquito repellent.

At the end of the week, both families used the light traps again. The day after that, Tomás and his mom visited the Woodsons so everyone could learn the results.

"There are many fewer mosquitoes in the trap this time," said Mr. Woodson. "Fantastic!"

Mrs. Woodson took out her notepad and ==did some calculations==. She smiled. "We caught less than half the number of mosquitoes, compared to what we caught last week."

"How are your bites?" Mrs. Littleton asked Mr. Woodson.

"Fine," he responded. "I've only had one or two bites in the past week. I have never had so few mosquito bites in the summer."

↖ Mr. Woodson couldn't believe how few mosquito bites he had gotten.

"Mom's ideas really helped!" said Tomás.

"The neighborhood is having a council meeting in a few days. I think we should share what we found with our study. We can show them our evidence that the methods work," said Mrs. Littleton.

"I agree. But I still wonder about one thing. Wouldn't the world be better off without mosquitoes?" asked Mrs. Woodson.

"A number of scientists have discussed that idea," replied Tomás's mother. "One argued that we should find a way to change male mosquitoes so they cannot **fertilize** eggs. These males would be released into the wild, and slowly the number of mosquitoes would drop. Some chemical companies are trying to develop stronger **pesticides** that would kill off mosquito species.

Pesticides can kill off large numbers of insects very quickly.

↰ Mosquito larvae are a source of food for certain fish species.

"However," continued Mrs. Littleton, "many people argue against killing off species. There is evidence that it can have a damaging effect on nature."

"What do you mean?" asked Mr. Woodson.

Tomás answered the question because he had discussed it with his mom many times before. "Many animal and insect species eat mosquitoes," he said. "Those species might die off if we kill mosquitoes."

"In addition, thousands of plant species that depend on mosquitoes to **pollinate** them might not survive," said Mrs. Littleton.

"I never thought of those things," said Mr. Woodson.

"Mom always says you shouldn't mess with Mother Nature," said Tomás.

INSECT REPELLENT NEET DEET

100% DIETHYLTOLUAMIDE
100 ml

Keep out of reach of children
For external use only

TRAVELLERS ESSENTIALS

Not every idea that scientists come up with is a good one. An idea might cause more problems than it solves. To make matters more complicated, it is difficult to know an idea's long-term effects ahead of time. What seems to be a good idea one day may prove to be a dangerous one years later.

One question that scientists are still trying to answer is, What is the best way to battle mosquitoes and the diseases they spread? The possible solution of wiping out mosquitoes completely is not the only idea under debate. Scientists are also studying insect repellent. A chemical called DEET has been around for decades. It has been proven to be very effective at keeping mosquitoes and other insects away. However, it may be harmful to the people who use it, particularly children. As a result, researchers are searching for safer ways to repel mosquitoes.

CHAPTER 5

CLEANING UP THE NEIGHBORHOOD

↰ The two families carefully reviewed their materials as they prepared to present their findings.

The Woodsons and the Littletons spent the next few days creating a presentation for the council meeting. They included the maps and made a chart to compare the number of mosquitoes caught in each yard with the light traps. Mrs. Littleton helped Mr. Woodson make a big poster listing all of the ways to keep mosquitoes away.

Three nights later, Tomás, his mother, and the Woodsons presented their ideas at the council meeting. A few of the neighbors had questions.

"I have heard that mosquitoes can spread diseases," began Mrs. Hill. "Is that true?"

Mrs. Littleton nodded. "Mosquitoes can carry about a dozen different diseases. Each disease is only carried by certain species of mosquitoes. You may have heard of **malaria** and **West Nile virus**. Malaria is a serious disease, but it is extremely rare in North America. The people who need to worry most about malaria are those who travel to countries where the disease is common.

"However, the West Nile virus is found here, and there are more cases each year. Most of the mosquitoes get the disease from infected birds,"

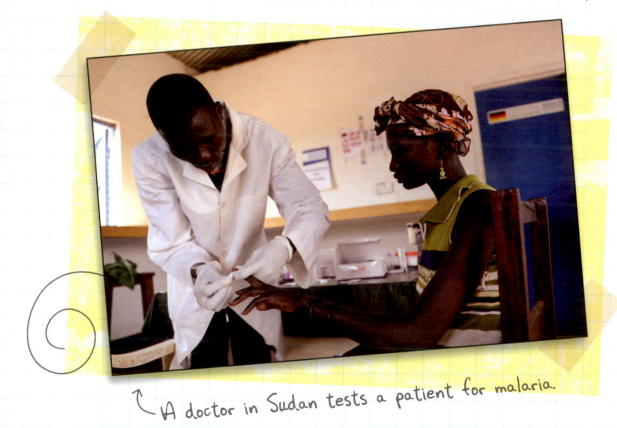

A doctor in Sudan tests a patient for malaria.

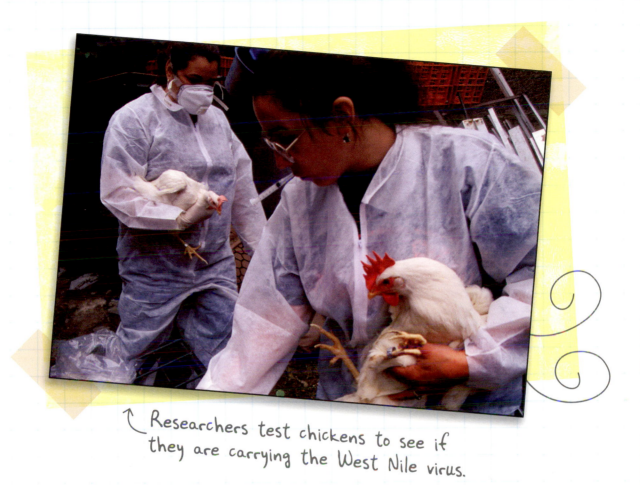

↱ Researchers test chickens to see if they are carrying the West Nile virus.

Mrs. Littleton explained. "Many people get the disease and never know it. That's because the **symptoms** of West Nile are the same as the flu. They include a fever, a stiff neck, and a headache."

Another neighbor, Mr. Larson, looked worried. "Can mosquitoes also infect animals, such as pets?"

"The most common disease to worry about with pets is heartworm," explained Mrs. Littleton. "This disease can affect dogs, cats, ferrets, and many animals found in the wild. Heartworm disease has been found in every state of the United States. A single bite from a mosquito is enough to infect an animal, although it often takes months for symptoms to

appear. Dogs are usually at the highest risk. Heartworm can be prevented with pills, shots, or liquid applied to the pet's skin."

"I think we should start a program to cut down on the number of mosquitoes in our area," responded Mr. Larson. Many other people at the meeting nodded. The council took a vote, and everyone voted to create the program.

"Well, Tomás, are you ready to help rid the neighborhood of pests?" asked Mr. Larson.

"Sure thing!" responded Tomás with a grin. "Are *you* ready?"

Pet owners give their dogs medicine to help prevent heartworm infections.

Mosquitoes are not the only creatures that can spread disease. Fleas and ticks may also carry illnesses. Fleas have been responsible for spreading the plague. This disease killed as many as 200 million people in Europe in the 14th century. Outbreaks today are largely limited to Africa, Asia, and South America. Ticks are related to spiders. They infect thousands of people every year. Two of the most common illnesses spread by ticks are Lyme disease and Rocky Mountain spotted fever.

The best way to combat these illnesses is knowledge. The better people understand a disease and how it spreads, the better they are at avoiding it. With this in mind, governments and organizations work to keep people informed about how to recognize a disease's symptoms. They also teach people how to avoid catching it and spreading it. Posters, Web sites, brochures, news reports, and even television shows all help keep the public in the know.

GLOSSARY

abdomen (AB-duh-muhn) the rear section of an insect's body

antennae (an-TEN-eye) a pair of sensory organs on an insect's head, which help it smell and feel

baseline (BASE-line) a line serving as a basis, as for measurement

entomologist (ehn-tih-MOL-uh-jist) a scientist who studies insects

fertilize (FUR-tuh-lize) to begin reproduction in an animal by causing a sperm cell to join with an egg cell

larvae (LAHR-vee) insects at the stage of development between an egg and a pupa, when they look like worms

malaria (muh-LAIR-ee-uh) a disease spread by a particular kind of mosquito, causing chills, fever, and sweating, and in extreme cases, death

pesticides (PES-ti-sydz) chemicals used to kill pests, such as insects

pollinate (PAH-luh-nate) to carry or transfer pollen from one flower to the same type, where female cells can be fertilized to produce seed

proboscis (pro-BOS-is) a slender, tubelike part of some insects' mouths

repellent (ri-PEL-uhnt) a chemical that wards off insects and other pests

symptoms (SIMP-tuhmz) signs of an illness

thorax (THOR-aks) the part of an insect's body between its head and its abdomen

West Nile virus (WEST NILE VYE-ruhs) a disease spread by mosquitoes that causes aches and pains, a skin rash, and nausea, and in extreme cases, death

FOR MORE INFORMATION

BOOKS

Abramovitz, Melissa. *West Nile Virus*. Detroit: Lucent Books, 2013.

Doudna, Kelly. *Mischievous Mosquitoes*. Minneapolis, Minn.: ABDO Publishing Company, 2012.

Markle, Sandra. *Mosquitoes: Tiny Insect Troublemakers*. Minneapolis, Minn.: Lerner Publications Company, 2008.

Owings, Lisa. *The Mosquito*. Minneapolis, Minn.: Bellwether Media, 2013.

Walker, Sally M. *Mosquitoes*. Minneapolis, Minn.: Lerner Publications Company, 2009.

WEB SITES

BioKids Critter Catalog—Mosquitos

www.biokids.umich.edu/critters/Culicidae

Read all about mosquitoes, from where they live to how they interact with humans.

National Geographic Kids—Mosquitoes

http://kids.nationalgeographic.com/kids/animals/creaturefeature/mosquitoes

Find facts, photos, videos, and more about mosquitoes.

TeensHealth—West Nile Virus

http://kidshealth.org/teen/infections/bacterial_viral/west_nile.html

Learn more about the West Nile Virus and how to protect yourself from it.

INDEX

ABOUT THE AUTHOR

Tamra B. Orr is an author living in the Pacific Northwest. She has a degree in Secondary Education and English from Ball State University. She is the mother of four children, and the author of more than 350 books for readers of all ages. When she isn't writing or reading books, she is writing letters to friends all over the world. Although fascinated by all aspects of science, she admits the idea of a world without mosquitoes is quite appealing.

A2170 685613 7